IT'S SHOW TIME
How to perform on television and radio

Companion guide
to the video program,
You're On The Air

Brian Jud

Cover by
Concialdi Design

Text layout by
Ellen Gregory

Edited by
Roberta J. Buland

© 1997, Brian Jud

First Edition

Published by Marketing Directions, Inc.

P. O. Box 715

Avon, CT 06001-0715

Other books by the Author:

Job Search 101
Perpetual Promotion
Resumes That Get Jobs
You're On The Air (Video)
The ABCs of Finding a Job
Preparing for the Interview
Coping With Unemployment
Help Wanted: Inquire Within
The Art of Interviewing (Video)
Writing Persuasive Cover Letters
Advanced Interviewing Techniques
Successful Interviewing Techniques
Elementos básicos para buscar trabajo
The ABCs of Coping With Unemployment
Effective Job-Search Telephone Techniques
The ABCs of Finding Prospective Employers
The Gold Book (Coauthor: Nadia Chudzik)

ISBN: 1-880218-26-7

Library of Congress Catalog Card Number: 97-092987

Table of Contents

Introduction

It's Show Time is the companion guide for the video program, *You're On The Air,* and is your manual for successfully performing on broadcast media.

The focus of *It's Show Time* is on television and radio appearances, but this does not undermine the need for an assortment of publicity-generating opportunities. You will be more successful if you implement a variety of appearances while you communicate one dominant theme: the uniqueness of your book, product or service.

The author of *It's Show Time* is Brian Jud, a veteran on the touring circuit, a syndicated columnist and a keynote speaker. He is also the president of Book Marketing Works, L.L.C., a company to help authors self-publish and market their books. Brian is also the host of the television series, *The Book Authority*, where he has hosted and produced over two hundred shows. In addition, he conducts self-publishing seminars and workshops and is the founder of the Connecticut Authors Association.

The information in *It's Show Time* comes from Brian's personal experience as well as interviews with industry professionals who tell you how to contact them and then give you inside tips on performing effectively when you are on the air. Here are the people you will be hearing from:

Jim Bohannon, host of the nationally broadcast *Jim Bohannon Show*

Dr. Wayne Dyer, author of *Your Erroneous Zones, The Sky's The Limit* and *Real Magic*

Rick Frishman, president of Planned Television Arts

Bill Granger, book publicist

Steve Hall, Publisher of "Radio-Television Interview Report"

Brad Hurtado, former producer of the television shows: *Donahue, Maury Povich* and *The Charlie Rose Show*

Larry Kahn, Director of Talk Programming at Westwood One Entertainment, the company that produces and distributes talk programming for *Larry King Live, David Brenner, Tom Leykis, Bruce Williams, Jim Bohannon, Imus in the Morning* and *G. Gordon Liddy*

Laura Kittell, Producer of *The Brad Davis Show,* WDRC-AM, Hartford, CT

Lori Dolney Levine, Senior Talent Executive, *Fox After Breakfast*

Eric Marcus, author of the #1 bestselling book, *Breaking the Surface* and former producer for *Good Morning America* and *CBS This Morning*

Patty Neger, producer of *Good Morning America*

Nick Peters, Vice President, Medialink, a company that produces satellite tours

Suzi Reynolds, professional media trainer

Rita Thompson, Field Producer for *CNBC, CBS News and Chronicle*

Deborah Wetzel, morning news anchor and talk-show host on WCBS-FM, New York City

Benita Zahn, noon news anchor and talk-show host on WNYT-TV, Albany, NY

You don't have to be a complete pro at performing on the air. What you simply need to do is know your audience, be familiar with your subject, understand what it is you're trying to accomplish and follow your instincts.
Nick Peters

Introduction

It's Show Time is the companion guide for the video program, *You're On The Air,* and is your manual for successfully performing on broadcast media.

The focus of *It's Show Time* is on television and radio appearances, but this does not undermine the need for an assortment of publicity-generating opportunities. You will be more successful if you implement a variety of appearances while you communicate one dominant theme: the uniqueness of your book, product or service.

The author of *It's Show Time* is Brian Jud, a veteran on the touring circuit, a syndicated columnist and a keynote speaker. He is also the president of Book Marketing Works, L.L.C., a company to help authors self-publish and market their books. Brian is also the host of the television series, *The Book Authority*, where he has hosted and produced over two hundred shows. In addition, he conducts self-publishing seminars and workshops and is the founder of the Connecticut Authors Association.

The information in *It's Show Time* comes from Brian's personal experience as well as interviews with industry professionals who tell you how to contact them and then give you inside tips on performing effectively when you are on the air. Here are the people you will be hearing from:

Jim Bohannon, host of the nationally broadcast *Jim Bohannon Show*

Dr. Wayne Dyer, author of *Your Erroneous Zones, The Sky's The Limit* and *Real Magic*

Rick Frishman, president of Planned Television Arts

Bill Granger, book publicist

Steve Hall, Publisher of "Radio-Television Interview Report"

Brad Hurtado, former producer of the television shows: *Donahue, Maury Povich* and *The Charlie Rose Show*

Larry Kahn, Director of Talk Programming at Westwood One Entertainment, the company that produces and distributes talk programming for *Larry King Live, David Brenner, Tom Leykis, Bruce Williams, Jim Bohannon, Imus in the Morning* and *G. Gordon Liddy*

Laura Kittell, Producer of *The Brad Davis Show,* WDRC-AM, Hartford, CT

Lori Dolney Levine, Senior Talent Executive, *Fox After Breakfast*

Eric Marcus, author of the #1 bestselling book, *Breaking the Surface* and former producer for *Good Morning America* and *CBS This Morning*

Patty Neger, producer of *Good Morning America*

Nick Peters, Vice President, Medialink, a company that produces satellite tours

Suzi Reynolds, professional media trainer

Rita Thompson, Field Producer for *CNBC, CBS News and Chronicle*

Deborah Wetzel, morning news anchor and talk-show host on WCBS-FM, New York City

Benita Zahn, noon news anchor and talk-show host on WNYT-TV, Albany, NY

> *You don't have to be a complete pro at performing on the air. What you simply need to do is know your audience, be familiar with your subject, understand what it is you're trying to accomplish and follow your instincts.*
>
> **Nick Peters**

Chapter One

CREATING PERSONAL MAGNETISM

Have you wondered why celebrities being interviewed on television can look so calm when millions of people are watching them? And have you ever wondered if you could do that?

You can appear on national television and radio, and you can appear calm and collected, just like the actors you see every day. But like actors, you can not just show up for performances. Actors learn their lines and rehearse them until they create a believable, entertaining performance. You can be successful, too, if you approach your media events the same way.

The key to any good performance is preparation. Just as actors do, media guests need to know what they are going to say during all their performances and practice their delivery of each word beforehand. Adequate preparation will make you more confident in your ability to perform and help you relax while you are on the air.

> *If you speak monotonously, it's nothing you're going to change in the 30 seconds before you go on the air. If you think you've got a terrible voice, go see a coach.*
> **Benita Zahn**

2 Creating Personal Magnetism

You have heard it said that practice makes perfect. However, that is not necessarily true. Practice makes *permanent*, so you have to make sure you are rehearsing the right things. Before you appear on any media event, engage the services of a professional media trainer so the techniques you make permanent are the right ones.

> *I have found that an author is not always ready to be interviewed. It is not just a matter of answering a few questions and plugging your 800 number.*
> **Bill Granger, Book Publicist**

Hiring a media trainer to coach you in performing successfully may be the best single investment you can make to conduct an effective appearance. Therefore, search carefully and retain the services of a seasoned media trainer. It is best to employ one early to discover where you need the most assistance and help you make corrections. Without the benefit of an experienced instructor, you can not be sure you are practicing the correct techniques.

> *Media training will give you relaxation, calm you down, make you understand how things operate, make it easy for you to do television. You won't be preoccupied with what is happening here or happening there. You'll be able to focus, and that's the most important thing.*
> **Lori Dolney Levine**

Professional media trainers can provide one-on-one or group sessions. Some will even serve as your publicist once your training is completed, helping you negotiate appearances on national television shows. A good media trainer will instruct you on conducting preshow preparation, applying makeup, wearing the right clothes, creating your presentation, using your voice well, gesturing convincingly and answering questions in a poised manner. Ask your coach to videotape your session for a complete record of what was said.

> *One author never understood why he didn't get more than three minutes on an interview and never sold any books. I said, "You're boring. Boring, boring, boring. And if you don't pay any attention to that, you aren't going to sell any more books. You asked me for my opinion, you're boring.*
>
> **Brad Hurtado**

Most people are not lucky enough to find someone who will give them honest feedback, so they keep making the same mistakes and never reach their goals.

Take two classes and call me in the morning

Practice on a regular basis and you will conduct professional and successful interviews. Your practice sessions can be as formal or informal as you want them to be. They run the gamut from talking into a cassette recorder to hiring a professional media trainer as a coach. One technique described by Benita Zahn is to have someone who knows nothing about your subject ask you questions. This simulates most interviews, and it will help you practice responding to unexpected questions. The important point is to do something every day to improve your media skills.

Good, better, guest

Practice can be as easy and fun as listening to or watching talk shows. On television, watch how successful guests interact with the host and audience. Try watching the show on which you are scheduled to appear, with the sound off to focus your attention on the guests. How do they sit? What do they wear? What are the seating arrangements and backgrounds? What are the predominant camera angles? Incorporate what you see into your own performance.

Turn the sound back on and listen to the host. How are questions asked? How does he or she stimulate audience participation? What is the pace of the show? On radio, listen to the interaction between guests and host and between guests and callers. What makes one show better than others? How are stories woven into the author's answers? Does the guest answer the host's questions directly or follow his or her own agenda?

Where to find a media coach

Consult the *Yellow Pages* to locate a local media trainer. If you live in the New York City area, contact Suzi Reynolds at 200 Rector Place, Suite 7H, New York, NY 10020, (212) 945-2071. Or you could reach a talk-show host or news anchorperson at a nearby station and contract for his or her services. For example, Benita Zahn is an excellent media trainer and can be reached at WNYT-TV, 15 North Pearl Street, Albany, NY 12204, (518) 436-8477.

Seek the local chapters of Toastmasters International and the National Speakers Association, or take a Dale Carnegie course. Go to your library and look at a directory called *The Encyclopedia of Associations* for a list of nearby writers groups. For example, the Connecticut Authors Association offers a full-day, media training course including an actual on-camera interview and professional critique of your performance. For more information, contact the CAA at P. O. Box 715, Avon, CT 06001-0715.

> *If the author needs media training it's usually not he or she who figures it out. The producer or publicist figures it out. Authors tend to think they're really good on their topic, but they may not be good storytellers.*
>
> **Brad Hurtado**

Chapter Two

TYPES OF SHOWS

You will be invited to appear on shows with different formats. These include talk shows, on which you will be the primary guest for your segment; news shows, where you will be interviewed for a few minutes; interviews at remote locations; and panel discussions, on which you will be one of several guests. Each format has its own requirements, so practice under all conditions.

Talk Shows

Talk shows, particularly those on television, have received mixed reviews. They have been denounced as the harbinger of tabloid sensationalism by some and proclaimed as the window through which we view life's realities by others. One can make a case for both positions, and some shows may fit into either category at different times. Those opinions notwithstanding, many talk shows educate viewers on the pros and cons of informative issues without resorting to melodrama.

★ Regardless of your opinion of talk shows in general, an appearance on one can make good business sense. You can reach thousands or millions of people for fifteen minutes or more for free. This can translate into increased recognition and sales.

6 Types of Shows

★ Talk-show producers book guests who have information of interest to their viewers. Their objective is to create a memorable, provocative show that will increase ratings.

> *A producer looks for story ideas, tries to find good interviews and pictures, then puts together a segment on the air. I have to think of the viewer first. It's not my job to sell books, but to make interesting television. If a book helps me get interesting television, that's good.*
>
> **Rita Thompson**

★ The decision not to select you may have nothing to do with your experience or topic. If your subject is not right for the audience or if the topic has been the theme of a recent show, the producer will opt for a different guest this time. If you are rejected, find out why and resubmit your proposal later.

> *There are ways in which you can find a sympathetic ear over the phone to tell you what went wrong with your book, what went right with your book, what missed and what hit.*
>
> **Brad Hurtado**

★ You will generally have more time on the air during a talk show than a news show, enabling you to include more points about your topic and your book.

★ There will be frequent commercial breaks, creating a natural transition between discussion topics. Talk with the host during the commercial to analyze what has happened so far and plan what you will discuss next.

★ Many television talk shows are performed before a live studio audience. If the host takes questions from the audience, interact with them. Never belittle a question, but do not be intimidated, either. The same principles apply to radio shows that permit people to call and ask you questions.

The bottom line of your appearance on a talk show is to conduct yourself in an informative, relaxed and entertaining manner. Create a memorable, positive experience for the audience and the host, but at the same time do what you must to reach your objective.

> *The most important thing, whether you're on a radio show or a television show, is to be an engaging guest. It's a performance. You have to think of yourself as an actor. You have to be an active participant.*
> **Eric Marcus**

News Shows

If your topic has something to do with a late-breaking local or national news event, you may be asked to appear on a news show. This interview could take place live in the studio, live at a remote location or taped as part of a story to be aired at a later time. These segments are generally shorter in duration than on talk shows, lasting from two to four minutes, and in most cases the questions will be related to the current news event.

8 Types of Shows

★ You will typically be led onto the set during a commercial break. The host(s) will probably be on the set already. There may be two hosts, so do not let that startle you. If the host seems preoccupied, it is because he or she may be listening to the director's comments via an ear microphone. If so, do not interrupt or expect undivided attention.

> *I make it a point never to talk to guests before I go on. Guests have a tendency to have one really good response in them. If they regurgitate that beforehand, when we go on the air the next response is never as good as the first.*
>
> **Jim Bohannon**

★ Your segment will usually begin with a description of an important news event or circumstance. You will be asked specific questions about the event, with 30 seconds or less allotted for each answer.

★ On television, your eye contact should be with the interviewer, not the camera. Watch interviews between professionals on news shows to see how they talk with each other. The cameras will move to get the best shot of you.

★ You have only a few minutes on the air to make your points, so use your time effectively. Chapter Five discusses this strategy in detail.

> *You've got to look at your book and say, "What's the most important thing I have to hit?" And you've got to say it in about two sentences. That's all the time you get.*
>
> **Lori Dolney Levine**

Remote Broadcasts

In some cases your performance will be live, but from a location outside the studio. The television interviewer may be the anchorperson of the news show, on camera in the studio. In this case, you will have a microphone placed in your ear so you can hear the questions. Make sure it is comfortable and secure. Your segment will be cut short if you have to hold your finger on the microphone to keep it in place or if the connection is poor. Look straight into the camera facing you, not at your image on the monitor. Answer the questions as you would if you were on the set with the interviewer.

> *You may find yourself in a situation where you are not in the same room as the interviewer. In this case, look into the camera; talk to the camera.*
> **Benita Zahn**

Under other circumstances you may be interviewed on location by a reporter with a hand-held microphone. He or she will hold it in front of your mouth and make any necessary adjustments. Speak directly into the microphone in your normal tone of voice and make your intended points. Your eye communication should be with the reporter, not the camera. When the journalist begins his or her summary, you may look into the camera.

> In live interviews your words are not edited. Never use any profanity, innuendoes, slurs, personal attacks or other comments that could be offensive to the viewers.

If your interview is taped as part of a feature story, it will be edited by the reporter to fit his or her viewpoint and available time. You have no control over how your views are presented, and some of your points may be misconstrued. There will be no corrections or apologies. But, you can minimize unintentional misrepresentation if you are specific and concise in your answers.

Panel Discussions

You may appear on a show with other guests, with several people to be interviewed together. Panel discussions create new challenges since you are sharing the limelight with others who may or may not be as accommodating as you.

THE PANEL INTERVIEW

You don't want to come to blows, but if you disagree, you can respectfully disagree, and that makes for better television.
Benita Zahn

Find out ahead of time if you will be on with others or by yourself so you will not be caught off guard when you walk on the set. If you are appearing with others, ask if it will be a point-counterpoint debate or discussion, or a sharing of information. In any event, do not be led into arguments for which you are not prepared. You may speak your mind, but make your points politely.

After the introductions, each of you will have the chance to make an opening statement, or a general question will be posed to begin the discussion. You will be asked to describe your position and then defend it against the questioning of panelists or callers with opposing views.

Wordy opponents

Those sharing the panel with you have their own agendas and may try to communicate them at your expense, particularly if your viewpoint is different from theirs. Do not allow yourself to be taken in by someone whose objective is to use you for his or her own purposes. Also, do not repeat an opposing theory, thereby playing into his or her hands. Play off the others' comments, making the transition into your agenda.

> *If you are part of a panel discussion, you have three tools to use. Tool number one, jump into the conversation. Tool number two, always get back to the main point, your point, of the conversation. And tool number three is don't lose any chances to add your wealth of knowledge.*
>
> **Brad Hurtado**

Be prepared for unexpected events. Authors have strong opinions about their topics, which is what compelled them to write their book in the first place. Strong opinions combined with the opportunity to present them to a large audience can lead to ego flexing. As the audience size increases, some guests sense they are on stage and play to the viewers. This may be expressed verbally,

challenging your concepts, research methods and/or sources. It may be displayed visually, with exaggerated facial expressions such as rolling eyes, shaking heads or arms crossed in defiance. Or it may be exhibited subtly, as the person taking the role of devil's advocate.

> *I like people to respond to each other. Mine is an interview program and I try to see to it that a balanced presentation is offered.*
>
> **Jim Bohannon**

This is not to imply that all panel interviews are antagonistic. Most are meant to educate the viewers and are conducted without conflict. You will prove to be the more knowledgeable, credible source of information if you are prepared and remain composed. Know your material. Have facts, figures and supporting quotations at your fingertips. Stay calm and offer irrefutable proof of your position.

> *If you're lucky you'll get five minutes. If you're really lucky, you'll get eight. And if you're really, really lucky you'll get* Oprah.
>
> **Lori Dolney Levine**

Chapter Three

THE BIG DAY ARRIVES

Within a week of your performance, call the producer to confirm the time you should arrive and to get detailed directions to the studio. If you are scheduled to be on an early-morning show in a distant city, consider arriving there the night before rather than the morning of your segment.

Always allow time for unexpected events. Traffic can be heavy, and accidents do occur, or you may be delayed by the need for a security pass to enter the studio. Plan to arrive at the studio at least 20 - 30 minutes before your airtime.

Relax as you approach the studio

As you drive to the studio, prepare your mind and your voice for your upcoming performance.

14 The Big Day Arrives

★ If you are about to perform on a radio show, listen to it as you drive to the station. If another guest is speaking on your topic, listen to what the host and callers say to him or her. Then when it is your turn, you can refer to those conversations.

★ Loosen up your voice by saying the vowels, each with a progressively deeper voice. Do this several times, then do it again placing an "M" before each vowel: "MA, ME, MI, MO, MU."

★ Stretch, alternately tightening and loosening your jaw muscles. Open your mouth as wide as you can, then relax it. Rotate your shoulders, and then relax them. Repeatedly tighten and loosen your fists.

★ Do not think about how nervous you are. Instead, think about what you will do and say during the interview. Convince yourself that you are well-prepared and can handle anything that might come up.

★ Create and repeat positive affirmations. Here are several examples:
   I am in control of my plan and my thoughts.
   I am happy and calm.
   I have high energy.
   I am a winner.
   I feel good about myself.
   I believe in myself.
   I succeed because I perform to the best of my ability.
   I am relaxed, confident and creative.
   I speak with confidence.
   I project the positive feelings I have about myself.
   I am confident in myself and in my ability to perform.

Once you arrive, you are onstage
   When you arrive at the studio, the producer will greet you and take you to the green room (where guests await their time on the air). From the moment he or she lays eyes on you, you are making an

impression, which can be either good or bad. The producer is deciding if you are a player or not, a person who will conduct a lively, entertaining segment for the audience.

> *The minute you get in the television or radio studio you are on, you are being sized up. You don't know if the guest before you didn't show up and they're thinking of giving you the entire show. They're checking you out all the time.*
>
> **Rick Frishman**

Let him or her know you brought a blank tape with you and would like a copy of the show. In most cases it will be made while you are talking, rather than duplicated later. Bring two extra copies of your book with you. If the television producer has not already done so, he or she can arrange to show it on the screen. Or you may be able to use it as a prop. Leave a copy with the receptionist who will receive calls after your performance and will use your book to answer questions. Always autograph your books when you leave them with anyone.

As the time approaches for your segment, someone will take you to the studio and direct you to your seat. You will be shown how to use the microphone if you do not know how. If you have questions about any procedures or equipment, ask them at this point.

It is always important to make a good impression because it may affect the way the host works with you during the interview. These hints will help you create the right image:

★ When the host arrives, relax, shake hands confidently and smile. Ask, "What can I do to help you make this a good show?" This makes you a co-host and demonstrates your confidence and flexibility.

16 The Big Day Arrives

★ Describe the major points you want to address, and point out the list of questions you have prepared (bring an extra copy of your list with you).

> *If you're going to prepare questions, you might as well write questions that are going to push your point of view.*
> **Jim Bohannon**

★ Decide who will say your toll-free number and when.

★ Tell the host how you want to be described on the air, for example, as author, publisher, consultant.

★ Ask how you can weave any local interest into your conversation.

★ Ask about the timing of the breaks and how long each will last.

> *I was told that the only way you could talk to everybody in America was to get on all the big talk shows. But all the big talk shows never heard of Wayne Dyer. So there's another way to talk to everybody in America and that's to go to everybody in America. Go on every little radio show in every town across the country. Most of them, like* AM Columbus *and* Good Morning Jacksonville, *if you've got a new avocado dip they'll put you on. Take the books with you. Just do it, and don't tell yourself, "I've got to struggle."*
> **Dr. Wayne Dyer**

Chapter Four

HOW TO ANSWER QUESTIONS: CHOOSING YOUR WORDS

The discussion between you and the interviewer should not come across as an interrogation. It should be a conversation between an inquisitive host seeking helpful information and a knowledgeable person giving it.

Your objective should be to romance your audience, not to sell to it. Let your passion demonstrate what your book can do, not what your book is. You are not selling books, but dreams and solutions to problems. Prove to the audience that you can help them change their lives in some positive way. Use examples and personal stories to show how your book will make them happier, more fulfilled and/or successful. Sell the fire in your gut, the belief in your topic that caused you to write your book in the first place.

You can accomplish this to the extent you manipulate the content and delivery of your communication. The content of your message is comprised of the words you choose, and is the subject of the next two chapters. Your delivery is based upon the way you vary your voice and use your body language to project and create the desired image. These techniques are described in Chapter Six and Chapter Eight.

The content of your message

You have been asked to be a guest on a show because you have information that is important or interesting to people in the audience. If you are to be taken seriously, they must endorse you as a credible source of information, then believe and accept what you are saying.

> *Good guests are people who believe in their subject and know what they want to say.*
> **Jim Bohannon**

The host of the show, through his personality or format, has developed a loyal following. Since you were chosen by the host, the audience expects you to deliver on the implied promise that you have information they can use. At the end of your interview, they should sit back and think, "I'm glad I tuned in today. That was interesting. I think I'll buy that book to learn more about it."

You elicit this response through the content of your message which is based upon two things. The first is your knowledge of the people with whom you will interact: the host and the people in the audience. They will not give you a second chance if you come across as unprepared, uninformed or condescending. They do not care how much you know until they know how much you care. The second is you have to know your material.

Know the participants

Three participants are involved with every talk show: the host, the audience and the guest. Each has a different role to play with a separate reason for participating. The host wants to use the timeliness or controversial nature of your topic to inform and entertain the audience. His or her objective is not to make you look good or bad, but to improve the show's ratings by providing important information (from the viewer's or listener's perspective) in an entertaining, controversial or stimulating way.

> *The hosts are not there to hurt or torpedo you. They've invited you because you have expertise to share with the audience and you have as much talent as the person interviewing you.*
> **Benita Zahn**

The audience is seeking entertainment, knowledge or a way to pass the time. People do not tune in to be sold something and resent the person who tries to impose unwanted information upon them. If you talk only about your book and why people should buy it, you probably will not influence many to do so.

> *A good guest is someone who knows the audience and who can answer questions without too much about "my book."*
> **Larry Kahn**

20 How To Answer Questions: Choosing Your Words

How effective would you be communicating to an audience worldwide if your message were broadcast only in English? Would you be more effective if it was translated into the language of each country? If you talk to any audience using words or terms it does not understand, you might as well be speaking in a foreign language. The audience will not know what you are talking about, and will tune you out or switch to another station.

> *Speak English and not jargon; one of the problems many people have is they're so into the details of the subject at hand they expect everybody to know the shorthand. If you're in the business you know what they are, but most of us don't.*
>
> **Benita Zahn**

Find out what language the audience speaks by learning the composition of the audience for each show on which you perform. Is it predominantly male or female? How old are they? What is the average level of education? What do they currently know about your topic and what do they need to know? If taped, when will your show air (for example, what will be the frame of mind of the listener or viewer)? The more you know about the people in your audience, the more you can impact them.

> *A good show for the audience is to have an interesting guest, a guest who has a passion for whatever he or she is talking about. The most important thing is that the guest be able to communicate, to speak in a way that attracts the audience's attention without a lot of jargon.*
>
> **Jim Bohannon**

Know your material

You will please the host, and the audience will pay attention to you, if you come across as a credible, knowledgeable source of information. To communicate effectively you should have logical, well-supported answers to the questions posed by the interviewers or callers, which you can do if you are thoroughly familiar with your subject matter. Read what others have said on your subject and reread your own book. This latter point may sound unnecessary because you wrote your book and you know what is in it. But before rejecting this, consider these points:

★ You will be surprised at how quickly you will forget details you wrote just six months ago. Your hosts and callers may have read it yesterday and will have detailed questions for you.

★ Become familiar with your table of contents and subheads. Producers and hosts who do not have time to read your entire book will take their questions from these.

> *Don't assume the host or producer has read your book. Most of the time they will work off your table of contents or suggested questions, and assume you'll take the ball and run with it.*
> **Rick Frishman**

★ Know what your competitors have said about the topics on which you (or they) have taken a stand. If your host or someone in the audience disagrees with something you wrote, or cites your competitor's position, be prepared to discuss your reasoning.

> *I don't go on as a guest. I go on as an expert.*
> **Eric Marcus**

You have two jobs in every performance. The first is to accomplish your goal and the second is to provide a good show for the audience. These do not always go hand in hand. It is a fine line to walk, but you have to answer the questions to the satisfaction of the audience and the host, and you have to do so in a way that also meets your objectives.

> *Get familiar with your information so you don't have to think about it. Then you can be in the moment. It frees you to respond to any stimulus.*
> **Suzi Reynolds**

How To meet multiple objectives

Your interview will meet the goals of all participants if you use your verbal flexibility to inform and entertain the audience. Use words to convince the host and audience that you have information that is important to them and you have *their* best interests in mind while at the same time communicating information about your book.

There are seven guidelines to help you do that. Use them whenever you talk on the air so you come across as:

1) Creative. An innovative approach gets and holds the attention of the audience. However, many people feel uncomfortable being creative because they think it is an outlandish departure from conventional techniques. Instead, think of it as a strategy for gaining and maintaining the attention of your audience. Since the viewers or listeners are preoccupied with other activities that distort or inhibit your intended message, you can break through to them quickly by being different, but in an entertaining way.

For example, introduce unexpected or new information. Give it a new angle on what is already known. Capture the imaginations of the people in the audience with a twist on what they anticipate, and you will have them in the palm of your hand.

For instance, Caroline Kennedy demonstrated creativity while promoting her book *The Right to Privacy* on the *Oprah Winfrey Show.* Caroline prepared a videotape describing the humiliation to which one woman was subjected while being interrogated by the police. The tape included an interview with the woman, who was also in the live audience. This multimedia presentation riveted the audience's attention on the discussion.

2) Credible. A guest is not looked upon as an objective spokesperson, and the audience naturally expects you to say only what is good about your book or product. To combat this impression, tell the host how you want to be described in your introduction. Are you an expert who has also written a book? Are you a consultant? Are you president of your own company? Give the host the words that will position you as an objective source of information.

Most hosts begin with a question to establish your credentials to let the audience know you have the qualifications to make statements about this topic and you should be taken seriously.

I ask the author to outline his or her credentials right away so my listeners know you went to Harvard or spent X years researching. It builds the author's credibility.
Deborah Wetzel

The perception of an ulterior motive makes you suspect in the viewers' minds immediately. Combat that by using real-life illustrations as Caroline Kennedy did. It can be more effective if the examples are personal, describing what you went through and expressing the feelings you experienced. Make the audience empathize with you. Show them how you survived (or conquered, implemented, discovered or proved) something and, by following your advice, how they can, too.

Proper grammar and a good vocabulary will make you appear more credible, too. Learn how to use English properly, and practice using different words to express yourself.

★ Don't allow non-words (such as "um, uh") to creep into your speech. Frequent use of "OK" and the words "you know" may also alienate the listener.

★ Guests can diminish their credibility before a mature audience by using expressions that are "hip" or "cool" in everyday speech, but rarely used in the business world. They also detract from communication effectiveness because the audience is focused on the idiom, not the essence of the message. Hence, the words "like" and "awesome" suggest you may not be the authority you say you are.

There is an element of presumed credibility in the fact that you are brought into the viewers' homes by a trusted friend: the host of the show. If the host treats you with respect, it creates an inherent, implied endorsement of your credibility. Build upon this by becoming part of the show as a co-host or one friend talking to another.

Respect the host in return. Do not try to make him or her look bad by saying (or insinuating) something negative such as, "You mean you don't know about that?" Instead, help your host out of a potentially embarrassing situation. Your hosts know the television business but may not know your subject as well as you do. Even if they do, they may ask very basic questions for the benefit of the audience.

> *I'm looking for people who are natural, someone with a sense of humor who can tell a good story. I look for a person who is not intimidating but can make intimidating information accessible to my viewers.*
>
> **Rita Thompson**

Avoid what Lori Dolney Levine calls "The Smart Factor," where you feel you have to impress the audience with how much you know. If you help people in some way, if you know what you are talking about, then you look smart. Let them know immediately that you are not there to try to impress them, but to help them overcome some problem they have or could have. Know who you are and speak from your heart.

> *It's not important to look smart. It's more important to look believable.*
>
> **Lori Dolney Levine**

3) Current. Little will damage your credibility as much as your bewildered look and vague answer in response to a host's question on a timely topic.

> *I like people who have done their homework. They know my audience and can relate their subject to a local event.*
>
> **Deb Wetzel**

26 How To Answer Questions: Choosing Your Words

Read national newspapers, magazines and watch news programs so you can respond to questions on late-breaking events. When performing on a show in a distant city, read its newspaper for local events pertaining to your subject.

> *Interviewers will talk about what they're getting over the wire services, not what's in your book.*
> **Suzi Reynolds**

Before going on the air, ask the host if there are any local issues which you can address during the interview. News shows are about news, so give current information related to events of importance.

> *You can put yourself at the head of the pack by relating your book to a current event.*
> **Deb Wetzel**

> *If you're not a local resident I don't expect you to know local events. And I don't expect you to be a walking encyclopedia. But I do expect you to know national events surrounding your topic, what pertains to the topic we're here to discuss.*
> **Benita Zahn**

4) Convincing. What is true is not always believable, and what is believable is not always true. Document your words. Provide enough details to convince the audience that you are telling the truth. For example, by having the subject of the tape in the live audience, Caroline Kennedy persuaded people to believe her story was real.

> *Let it sink into the audience. Don't try to say too much.*
> *Mentally edit so you work with the audience, giving them*
> *time to understand what you are saying.*
>
> **Suzi Reynolds**

You can present charts and figures to document what you say, but doing so is not always helpful or necessary (particularly on radio). Instead, win your audience over by using the following fourteen words proven to elicit a positive response: *you, free, discover, safety, help, results, money, save, guarantee, health, new, proven, love* and *easy.* Using these words will convince the audience you are on its side, interested in helping it discover a new, easy way to save money or achieve other proven results. Members of the audience will love you for the free information; guaranteed.

> *I think it's very important that an author should be*
> *able to tell good anecdotes, bring a story to life. I'm not*
> *interested in statistics. I'm not interested in knowing how*
> *intellectual you are. I want you to be able to touch my*
> *viewer.*
>
> **Rita Thompson**

Watch your host for an indication of the extent to which you sound convincing. He or she will (intentionally or unintentionally) give signs of rapt attention, skepticism, indifference or outright objection. Look for the host's head nodding in agreement

or shaking in disbelief, a questioning scratch on the back of the head or frequent glances at the studio clock. Do not overreact to any one signal, but look for indications of your progress. Ask for feedback and make any necessary adjustments.

5) Complete. The length of a complete answer is relative. If you are on a news show for three minutes, you do not have time to develop a long response. Your answer should be a complete thought, condensed to fifteen or twenty seconds. The host will prompt you if more information is needed for clarification or substantiation.

> *I don't want a filibuster, but I don't want a yes or no answer either.*
> **Jim Bohannon**
>
> *The length of an answer in a two-minute news segment should probably be about 15-20 seconds. Just get to the heart of it.*
> **Benita Zahn**

If you are on a half-hour talk show, you have more opportunity to develop your answers. But do not make them too long, and always keep the host and audience involved in your response so it does not turn into a boring monologue.

> *A good guest is an engaging guest. Lively. Funny, if appropriate. Someone who knows the length of the show and can adjust the length of their answers accordingly.*
> **Eric Marcus**

The more organized your response, the less likely you are to ramble. Construct answers using anecdotes to prove your point.

> *Always give your answer in three parts. State the problem, an example of the problem that everyone can understand and relate to, and then the solution. Make them say at the end of the day, "Yeah, I learned something."*
> **Rick Frishman**

Below are four ways to structure your answers. Use one or more of them during a show to vary your responses, build rapport and make the interview seem like a conversation:

The chronological response. This method involves a description of your subject from a strategic beginning point. Starting with the earliest relevant experience, describe each event before moving on to the next. Or you could use the reverse-chronological sequence beginning with your most current information and then going backward in time.

The narrative response. This format gives you the chance to present your point in the form of a story. Use a narrative response only during shows of fifteen minutes or more. It is a good response to the amiable host seeking information about the real you, the person behind the image.

The enumerative response. This is a good technique to use in a short segment, when the host asks for "three quick examples to prove your point." List and describe each briefly, counting them off on your fingers for emphasis. You could also use the enumerative technique at the end of the show to summarize your agenda items.

> *Bullet-point your chapters. Come up with catch phrases that summarize what you're trying to say.*
> **Suzi Reynolds**

The geographical response. Use this style when it is important to describe *where* something took place.

Do not think that by speaking faster you will be able to get all your points across. It does not work that way. Just use ordinary, everyday communication skills and make your points interesting.

> *The rules are pretty much the rules of common, ordinary communication. Speak as if you were giving a talk to your boss or talking to the Rotary Club.*
> **Jim Bohannon**

Provide the right amount of information, interesting the viewer in what you are saying in the time allotted for your segment. Relate to the people listening or watching and give them a reason to continue.

6) Clear. Do not beat around the bush. People listen to the radio and watch television while doing something else. Get their attention with an immediate, positive impact so they heed what you are saying.

> *Figure you're talking to someone who knows nothing about your topic. Pretend you're talking to a ten-year old. Remember, people are not sitting still, hanging on your every word.*
> **Benita Zahn**

> *This is not the printed page. If you miss something, it's gone forever. Speak in a way that enables people to understand you.*
>
> **Jim Bohannon**

> *I want somebody who is going to be concise, clear and accessible. Someone who can take perhaps complicated information and put it in very simple, understandable terms.*
>
> **Rita Thompson**

You are the expert on the topic under discussion. That is why you were asked to be on the show. Translate your message so the audience can understand what you are saying. Make simple, direct answers that are understandable to the lowest common denominator. Be natural, friendly and informative. Smile to show you enjoy the experience.

7) Concise. Make every word count.

> *A good guest is one who speaks clearly about the subject, gets the point across in less words, not more.*
>
> **Lori Dolney Levine**

> *Some people don't understand the word concise. Make your point in 15 seconds. Learn how to speak for television; you don't have time to set up your answer. Give your answers in complete thoughts in a concise amount of time. Don't digress to other points and don't ramble.*
>
> **Rita Thompson**

People filter out anything they feel is irrelevant, but listen more intently if something seems to be important to them. It is not difficult to take part in an interview if you know and believe in your message.

> *We're looking for someone who is not boring but who doesn't talk too much. Someone who gets to the point. Someone who can speak clearly, naturally and someone who can address the questions that the host asks.*
>
> **Larry Kahn**

Chapter Five

GET YOUR WORDS' WORTH

Two concepts determine your relative success in answering questions: preparation and flexibility. You may or may not know the questions you will be asked, nor the person asking them. But if you know your topic and know what you want to get across to the audience, you will be able to perform more than adequately in any situation.

What makes a good guest for the show does not always make a good show for the guest. If all you do is answer the interviewer's questions informatively (whether or not they lead to meeting your goals), the host will think you are a great interviewee and perhaps ask you to return. But there is no future in being a professional guest if you do not sell your books in the process.

It's like Jeopardy. *Think, "Here's the answer. Now, what was the question?"*
Suzi Reynolds

Your objective may seem at odds with those of the host and audience. But it does not have to be. You can reach your goals as you help others reach theirs if you provide information in an entertaining way, stimulating them to purchase your book for more details. As a general rule, you will sell more books if you entertain people, piquing their curiosity, showing them how they can reach their goals by using the information in your book.

> *The guest has to keep in mind that he or she has two jobs. One is to sell books, a concept, a political cause, whatever. The other is to provide a good show. The two don't necessarily run in parallel.*
>
> **Jim Bohannon**

Convincing people to do something they had no intention of doing takes strategy, preparation and finesse. You have to charm the audience while communicating important information about your book. And you may have to do it in three minutes, perhaps while the host is asking you questions that may have nothing to do with what you want to say. Reaching your goals under these conditions requires that you blend your understanding of the audience, knowledge of your topic, diplomacy and training to create a polished, effective performance.

> *You have to give information. But you also have to make them fall in love with you and that's what is going to make them buy your book.*
>
> **Rick Frishman**

The trick is to go into the interview knowing what you have to say and work that information into the conversation (with tact and diplomacy) regardless of what the questions are.

> *Producers know why you're on the show. You're not just doing it because you want to help the station, and everybody understands the rules. Answer the questions, but select one, two or three key messages you're trying to get across during the course of the interview and find ways to weave those into the answers to the questions you can expect to get.*
>
> **Nick Peters**

This does not mean you ignore the interviewer's questions totally and recite what you think they need to know. That might cause the host and the audience to become indignant. Instead, allow the host time to fulfill his or her agenda (being a good interviewer) to the extent that your purpose is not compromised. If you sense the conversation going off in a different direction and you have not addressed your critical points, you must begin to respond differently.

> *If the interviewer asks what you really aren't comfortable with and you really believe you need to be somewhere else, touch on the initial question and go to where you want to be. At least pay lip service to that initial question and move into your area by saying, "That's a fine question, Brian, but if we put it in the context of...." Now I've acknowledged it, complemented the interviewer and got it to where I want to be. If you don't answer, it will look as if you're evading the question.*
>
> **Benita Zahn**

Become proficient at acknowledging the host's questions and perhaps even answering them briefly, leading into your agenda items.

> *Periodically validate the host. It prepares the audience that you've got something to say that's important.*
> **Suzi Reynolds**

You can do this if you know the answers to these questions:

★ Given a limited time on the air, what information do you want to impress upon the audience?

★ What are the major points you must communicate? The number of unique points you can communicate effectively depends upon the length of time you have on the air, making fewer in a three-minute interview than in a half-hour segment. Since you will participate in shows of varying lengths, decide in advance how many points you can communicate reasonably in a variety of different time periods.

> *You have to package yourself into the time you have available. If you have one hour on a radio show, there's plenty of time. But if you've got three minutes on a national show, in a short amount of time, you have to hit the ball out of the park.*
> **Brad Hurtado**

★ What information is important to each audience? Your agenda points will change, depending upon the composition of the people listening or viewing. Make sure you talk about what is important to the audience of each show.

> *You have to give the audience at least three things to do today that will change their lives, or their husbands' lives or their children's lives. But you have to hit home and you can't tease.*
>
> **Rick Frishman**

★ In what order should you discuss your agenda items? Avoid the temptation to say everything you know. People can not remember too many things at one time, so communicate the information most likely to gain the attention and interest of the audience as it relates to your ultimate objective.

> *Give people information in clusters of three. Even if you have nine points, give them in groups of three.*
>
> **Suzi Reynolds**
>
> *Most of the time what interviewers are looking for are three big points. Understand that before going in. When they ask, "So, what are the big issues here?" you can say A, B and C. Now you've begun to manage your interviewers. You've steered them into an area without making them feel foolish, without dictating terms per se. They want to bring out the best in you, and they want to look their best, too.*
>
> **Benita Zahn**

Succeed through planned spontaneity

Your success depends upon your ability to make a brief, yet smooth, transition from an irrelevant question (from your perspective) to one of your agenda items, making it relevant to the audience and not offensive to your host. Then once you make the transition, give an example to demonstrate your point. Concise, seemingly spontaneous illustrations, particularly those germane to the audience, can make your presentation more personable and convincing. People like to hear examples to which they can relate.

> *Producers want a good segment, but sometimes you have to get the discussion back to where you want it. It may not come off as planned, but if it's a good show, it's still good television.*
> **Lori Dolney Levine**

> *It is incumbent upon the talent to be prepared to either answer the tough or unexpected question or know how to deflect it.*
> **Nick Peters**

But this must be done cautiously. In a three-minute interview on a national show you do not have time to relate a complete story, and it can be embarrassing if the host cuts you off to end the segment or to stop you from rambling.

> *Answer the questions asked of you and let the host take the lead. Follow that lead and gauge from the environment of the show how much you can get in.*
> **Larry Kahn**

Creating your transition statements

Before you go on any shows, plan how you will use transition statements to lead the conversation back from an irrelevant question to one of the points you feel compelled to make. Then for each transition statement, create an example you can use to illustrate your agenda item. Here is a framework you can use to help organize your thoughts:

Agenda Item(s)	Transition Statements	Examples
3 minutes (Top three points)		
1)	1)	1)
2)	2)	2)
3)	3)	3)
7-minutes (Next three most important points)		
4)	4)	4)
5)	5)	5)
6)	6)	6)
15-minutes (Next three most important points)		
7)	7)	7)
8)	8)	8)
9)	9)	9)

30-minute show	During a show longer than fifteen minutes you will have more flexibility in your answers. You will be able to expand upon the interviewer's questions more leisurely while still covering your agenda items.

Use memory aids

There is a big difference between hearing something and listening to it. Hearing is a physical process and listening is a mental process. Hearing occurs when airwaves cause the bones in the middle ear to vibrate, transferring that sensation into the inner ear and then to the brain. Listening occurs when sounds are heard and understood. People can hear what you say without listening to you.

> *Listen to the person who is interviewing you. If they pick up on something neat you say you can go with the ball that they toss back in your court.*
>
> **Benita Zahn**

It makes no difference how good your performance is if the audience misinterprets what you say. Make your presentation clear by breaking through the listeners' or viewers' mental filters, gaining their attention and making them realize you are saying something important to them. A great way to do this is by creating memory aids to illustrate your point and make people remember your message. These aids can:

★ Help you organize your responses and present your information logically.

★ Help others remember what they heard.

★ Enable you to make a concise summary, leaving the audience with a few words to remember the content of your performance.

★ If your mind goes blank and you lose your train of thought, you can automatically speak about one of these familiar aids until you get back on track.

An *acronym* is one such memory aid. It is a word formed from the initial letters of a series of words, and you can use these to make an effective transition to your agenda items. For instance, here are examples of three acronyms:

PIE: A job search can be simple if the unemployed person **P**lans, **I**mplements and **E**valuates his or her campaign.

FEAR: Despondent job seekers should control their **FEAR** which represents their **F**inances, **E**motions, **A**ctions and subsequently their **R**esults.

DEAR: Job hunters can become DEAR to themselves by **D**iscovering, **E**mpowering, **A**ccepting and **R**especting themselves.

Here is how these acronyms are used to communicate your agenda items during a fifteen-minute appearance:

Major Points	Transition Statement	Example
1) PIE	People do not realize the job search is as simple as **PIE** if they *plan, implement* and *evaluate* it.	The letter **P** stands for the word **Plan**. For example, in the past I sent my resume to the people advertising in the newspaper and waited for a response. Then I...
2) *FEAR*	Many people begin to worry as soon as they are laid off. Instead, they should learn to control their **FEAR** and apply their energy in a positive way.	To demonstrate what I mean, let's look at the first word. People can control their finances by ...
3) **DEAR**	Continuous rejection in a job search can make people lose their self-esteem. To keep this f⁻om happening, people must become **DEAR** to themselves.	For example, before applying for a position, the job seeker must discover what he or she wants...

> *Don't use acronyms if you haven't explained them.*
> **Benita Zahn**

Avoid a quibbling rivalry

Here is an example of how these could be used during an interview:

Host: *What is the biggest mistake people make in their search for employment?*

Guest: The fatal mistake most job seekers make is not planning their search before they start. This may surprise your viewers, but the job search is as simple as *PIE*. This is an acronym to show people they must plan their campaign before they implement their actions. Then they must evaluate their progress to make sure they are heading in the right direction. The letter "P" stands for the word *Plan*. For example, in the past I simply sent my resume to the people advertising in the newspaper and waited for a response. Then I learned....

Host (*trying to change the direction of the interview*): *It's easy for you to say it's as simple as pie, but what do you tell the person who has just been laid off and is afraid of what might happen?*

Guest: That's a good point. Many people begin to worry as soon as they are laid off. Instead, they should learn to control their *FEAR* and apply their energy in a positive way. This is another acronym to remind people to control their finances, emotions, actions and subsequently their results. To demonstrate what I mean, let's look at the first word in this acronym. People can control their finances by ...

Host: *That all sounds nice, but doesn't the constant barrage of rejection drive an unemployed person's attitude into the ground?*

Guest: That's an excellent point. Continuous rejection in a job search can make people lose their self-esteem. To keep this from happening, people must become *DEAR* to themselves. Before applying for a position, the job seeker must discover what he or she wants to do ...

Host: *Well, Brian, our time is about up. Could you summarize before we close?*

Guest: *Y*our viewers should remember that their job search can be as simple as *PIE* if they just learn to control their *FEAR* and become *DEAR* to themselves.

If the host gives you an opening to summarize, just go back over your three big points and then you say, "Thank you" and you graciously leave.
Benita Zahn

Use comparisons, too

There are other devices you can use to make your answers compelling, including comparisons. Comparisons show similarity in some respects between things otherwise dissimilar. Use them to help illustrate your points. You can make a comparison by using a simile (a figure of speech comparing two unlike things by the use of the introductory *like* or *as*) or a metaphor (a figure of speech comparing two unlike things without using the introductory *like* or *as*).

Example of a simile: When explaining the *Implementation* portion of the PIE acronym, a simile can describe unconventional places to search for job opportunities. Begin by saying, "The job market is like an iceberg, which has only 10 - 15% of its mass visible. The remaining 85 - 90% is under water and not easily seen.

Similarly, in the job market, opportunities listed in the help-wanted ads represent only 10 to 15% of the positions available."

Example of a metaphor: While discussing the opportunities resulting from a layoff, one could begin by saying unemployment is the "dawn of a new day." Then proceed to talk about the positive aspects of job transition.

Simple is the way to go. You tell 'em what you're going to tell 'em. Then you tell 'em. Then you tell 'em what you told 'em.

Rick Frishman

Chapter Six

HOW TO ANSWER QUESTIONS: DELIVERING YOUR WORDS

The content of your message by itself does not guarantee effective communication. The key to a spontaneous, relaxed, entertaining and informative interview is to know your material and deliver it effectively, believably and passionately. The people in the audience will listen to you more intently if you gain and maintain their attention by manipulating the volume, pitch and tone of your voice.

A good guest is someone who can speak passionately, a person who communicates with the audience.

Jim Bohannon

We hear you loud and clear

As discussed in Chapter Five, an acronym will help you emphasize and articulate important words to deliver them more effectively. The acronym, VOICES, is made up of the first letter of the words **V**olume, **O**ther's viewpoint, **I**nflection, **C**onfidence, **E**nthusiasm and **S**peed. Vary these as you speak to deliver your message more effectively and pleasantly:

Volume. Before your segment begins, a sound check will be conducted and the audio controls will be adjusted accordingly. However, your general apprehension might make you feel less sure of yourself, and your voice may become progressively louder or softer. If this occurs, the host will mention it during a break. Or, if time is short, you may see the host or producer alerting you via hand signals to adjust your volume.

★ One or both hands, with palm(s) up, in upward motion means speak more loudly, or more quickly.

★ One or both hands, with palm(s) down, in a downward motion means speak softer, or more slowly.

> *I want people who are animated, with a loud voice but not screaming, articulate but not pompous.*
> **Lori Dolney Levine**

Others' viewpoints. The audience did not tune in to be sold something. It does not care about you and your book, but wants to be entertained or informed. Engage audience members by involving them in your presentation; convince them it is to their benefit to learn more.

> *People are always looking for help. It's one thing they can never get enough of. People are saying, "Help me, help me, help me."*
> **Lori Dolney Levine**

> *You may be selling the best product in the world, but if it doesn't apply to me, I'm not interested. I don't care. It doesn't matter what you're saying. It doesn't matter if you're the most beautiful person in the world. If it doesn't apply to me I'm not interested.*
> **Benita Zahn**

*I*nflection. Avoid a monotonous tone of voice by accenting important words, emphasizing them as you speak. Alter the way you accentuate your words so you control their impact. Adjust your volume periodically to emphasize important points and to avoid talking in a monotone.

> *It's helpful that people be able to speak in a manner which is persuasive, with appropriate inflection.*
> **Jim Bohannon**

> *Good guests are people who use their entire vocal range and use their hands as expressive tools. They are people who are not boring.*
> **Brad Hurtado**

*C*onfidence. People associate competence with confidence. If you sound confident, the audience is more likely to believe you know what you are talking about. The sound of confidence is not necessarily a deep, resonant voice. It is also a ready answer to a tough question or a command of the facts supporting your position.

> *You get someone's attention by being confident. You bring a presence to the screen because you're confident, not cocky. You'll fill the screen and your voice carries.*
>
> **Benita Zahn**

Perhaps the most effective way to exude confidence is through preparation and a good working knowledge of your subject.

> *People are most comfortable when talking about something they love, when they are talking about something they really believe in and are passionate about.*
>
> **Deb Wetzel**

But if you experience nervousness, there are several techniques you can use to project confidence:

★ Listen to the interviewer's questions carefully, giving yourself time to think of an answer.

★ Do not be afraid to say, "I don't know " or "I can't recall," if you do not or can not. Some questions are meant to throw you off balance to see if you really know what you are talking about (but these are usually asked by the host before you go on the air, if they occur at all).

★ Breathing exercises can help alleviate anxiety. A technique told by Kathy Wyler (WRCH-FM, Hartford, CT) is to picture a birthday cake on a table in front of you with hundreds of candles on it. Your job is to blow them all out, Take a deep breath and exhale with your mouth wide open. Repeat this a few times before the show starts, but do not overdo this exercise or you could hyperventilate.

> *If you get a case of the jitters while you're on the air, breathe in and hold your breath while the host is talking.*
> **Suzi Reynolds**

★ To the extent necessary, your hosts will try to make you feel at home. They recognize that you are apprehensive about appearing on the show, and they will do what they can to help you relax. Do not worry about the mechanics of the equipment. Your hosts will show you how to place the microphone and how to sit. If you have any questions, ask them before the show begins.

> *You already have to worry about what your central message is and the like. Don't worry about problems that don't concern you.*
> **Jim Bohannon**

> *Some authors are doing this for the first time, and I understand that. I'd rather have the guest feel comfortable and relaxed because I get a much better interview. I tell him to sit down and get comfortable. Then I'll position the microphone and we'll talk for a few minutes.*
>
> **Deborah Wetzel**

★ Do not think about your spouse, family and friends in the audience. Think about the questions and how you will use them to address your agenda.

★ Be yourself. Speak naturally and use personal stories to create camaraderie with the audience. Do not try to tell a joke if you feel nervous. It is less likely to go over well, and the lack of laughter will make you even more apprehensive.

> *Some people are just not funny, and if they try to be humorous they fall flat on their faces.*
>
> **Benita Zahn**

> *A technique used by professional speakers is to ground yourself by sitting with both feet flat on the floor. I also suggest you eat a light, high-fiber meal before the show, but nothing fatty or heavy with protein.*
>
> **Mary Sandro, National Speakers Association**

★ People are rooting for you to succeed. They empathize with your fallibility and may support you more if you prove yourself human. Do not worry about making a mistake because it can make for a better interview. Learn to laugh with yourself.

★ Many studios have a cough button on the console. If you must cough or clear your throat, press this as you do so and it will not be heard over the air. If there is no cough button, turn away from the microphone and cover your mouth.

> *I tell my guests just to turn their mouth away from the microphone to cough. It's not going to distract from the interview and it makes you sound more like a normal person. Everybody has to clear his or her throat at some point.*
>
> **Deb Wetzel**

★ The audience is less aware of your nervousness than you are. Do not call attention to it on the air, but if you feel it necessary, admit it to the interviewer before the show begins. This will help you relax, as well as build rapport.

★ Relax and enjoy yourself, but do not get too comfortable and make flippant remarks. Maintain your professionalism and think about what you are going to say before you say it. If you are unsure if a comment will be suitable, do not say it. As the saying goes, "If in doubt, leave it out."

Smile though your heart is quaking

Keep smiling even though you are nervous. Most of the time the audience will not know the difference. Practice smiling naturally in front of a mirror so you get a feel for what it is like. You may be surprised to see that sometimes when you think you are smiling, your face does not show it.

Take care of your teeth and your smile will look much better. Have them cleaned regularly and brush daily. Your smile will make the audience more confident in you, and you in yourself. You will look better and perform your best.

> *I'm always telling people. "It's not as bad as going to the dentist."*
> **Rita Thompson**

E **nthusiasm.** Temper your self-confidence with enthusiasm, communicated by speaking with a smile in your voice and passion in your heart. Use inflection to project enthusiasm as you accent important words.

> *You've got to make them say WOW!*
> **Brad Hurtado**

S **peed.** Your general anxiety may also cause you to speak more quickly than you would normally, distorting your articulation and interfering with effective communication.

> *You don't want to speak too rapidly. Remember that people may be picking you up over static or while driving in their cars.*
>
> **Jim Bohannon**

The normal rate of speech is about 130 - 140 words per minute. You can learn where you fit on this scale by counting 130 words. Time yourself saying them. If you speak too quickly or too slowly, practice until you get a good feel for your most comfortable and effective rate. You may see these hand signals relating to your rate of speech:

★ Two hands moving away from each other in a horizontal movement that looks like pulling taffy: keep talking. There is more time to fill before the break or end of show.

★ Index finger rotating: speed up, time is running out (the faster the motion, the less time you have). Wrap up quickly and let the host take over.

★ Index finger or hand brought across the throat: time is up! Stop talking immediately!

> *Practice speaking with punctuation. It gives the audience a mental break so they can understand and internalize what you said.*
>
> **Suzi Reynolds**

Boise will be Boise

Accept every opportunity to perform on television and radio. Tape and critique each to improve the content and delivery of your message. Practice the techniques for performing successfully and you will begin to feel at ease when you are on the air. Later, when you are invited to appear on a national radio show with millions of people in the audience, you will perform at your best. As Rick Frishman says, "Get really good in Idaho and then go for *Good Morning America*."

> *While you're on the air it would be a mistake to try to think about speaking up and speaking down and getting your information across and waving your hands. You're going to look like a clown. The best thing is to know your information, look the interviewer in the eye and believe in what you're saying.*
>
> **Benita Zahn**

Chapter Seven

SPECIAL HINTS FOR PERFORMING ON RADIO

Performances on radio talk or news shows are the workhorses of book-promotion activities. They provide reach (the number of people contacted), frequency (repetition of contact) and the flexibility to address a well-defined audience. With radio as part of your communication plan, you can reach hundreds, thousands or millions of people at little or no cost.

> *There are many benefits for anyone who wants to be on a radio talk program. You have a very engaged and involved audience. They really do pay attention.*
> **Jim Bohannon**

Radio appearances can be particularly beneficial if your message can be communicated without visuals. Radio is usually less nerve-racking than performing on television since you can use notes to aid your memory. In addition, you may be allotted more time per show (sometimes up to two hours) to get your information across. In many cases you can take telephone calls from listeners, and you can tape or perform your show live at the studio, from a remote location or over the telephone from home.

> *When I decide to have an author on, what I look for is someone who can relate to my audience, someone who feels passionate about the book, someone who can come in with the listener in mind, thinking about the person who has a radio on, listening for advice.*
> **Deb Wetzel**

Taped Radio Shows

Taped interviews to be aired later are produced at a time convenient to both the host and the author. Since you are not working under the pressure imposed by a live show's schedule, there is more time for you and your host to plan the topics to be discussed.

You will find radio appearances are enjoyable events, performed in comfortable clothes at the studio or from your home. There are other benefits to taped radio shows.

★ You will usually have more time devoted to your message.

★ There will be no calls from listeners (this can be a positive or a negative feature, depending on your goals and personality).

★ Guests fearing a contentious host feel more at ease while taping. If the interviewer becomes argumentative, you can stop talking and voice your concerns.

★ If you blunder or lose your place during the taping, the host can stop the tape and delete that part.

★ Taped shows can be rebroadcast. If your topic is evergreen (always relevant) and if your performance is adequate and not time sensitive (for example, if you do not mention something that dates your conversation), your show may be played again in the future.

Live Radio Shows

Live radio performances occur on talk shows, on newscasts and on regular programming. Although it is possible to perform live via telephone, it is better to broadcast from the studio whenever possible. This will give you the chance to network with the station's personalities and you are more likely to get additional airtime. Live radio shows can help you in these ways:

★ The increased tension of live performances can actually improve your performance. Since you must answer the questions as asked (with no chance to tape over mistakes), you will probably prepare more carefully and answer questions better, so you will sound more knowledgeable and spontaneous.

★ You can be more specific about dates and times of an upcoming event. It could be the impending release date of your book or a personal appearance later that day. The host wants to make the show sound current and relevant, and your specificity will contribute to that outcome.

★ Your time on the air could be extended. The host may ask you to return after a scheduled break if you are an entertaining speaker, if your performance is generating many calls, or if the next guest fails to show up.

If you do a morning drive radio tour you'll reach, on average, double what you have with a Today Show, *you'll have at least ten minutes of time to get your point across and you'll hit the right types of people.*
Rick Frishman

Hints for performing at your best

★ Feel comfortable and know what you are talking about.

> *Once the interviewer sits you down, you don't want to be stiff, but you don't want to move around talking on one side of the microphone and then the other. If that happens your voice levels are going to be all over the place. Just try to stay in one spot.*
>
> **Deb Wetzel**

★ Sit with your mouth 2 to 3 inches from the microphone and speak directly into it. Be careful that you do not accentuate your Ps" or whistle on your "Ss" although most microphones have a protective cover to minimize these plosive sounds.

> *Some microphones like that you treat them fairly closely and head on. Other microphones may like that you speak to one side. A good host or producer will tell you what it is you are supposed to do, so I wouldn't worry about it.*
>
> **Jim Bohannon**

★ If there are two or more hosts, continue speaking into the microphone as you turn your head to redirect your eye communication with the one asking the question. If you turn your head away from the microphone to speak to him or her, you will lose volume.

> *Don't look down. It's distracting to me and it takes away from the interview if you're not able to make eye contact. If you're nervous about doing the interview, don't be. It's really painless.*
>
> **Deborah Wetzel**

★ One advantage of radio over television is your book will be in front of you as you speak. But you will lose credibility if you take time searching for a particular quotation or fact to substantiate your point. Facilitate your search by using bright-colored sticky notes and markers to highlight major passages to which you can refer quickly. This will save time searching for the information while under pressure to respond. If you stop speaking while searching for the appropriate detail, the host will interject with his or her opinion on the topic. One thing the host will not allow is dead air (periods of silence).

> *There are two things a guest can do to really destroy the show. The first is to give only yes or no answers. The other is to come in, laden with papers, and shuffle through them before answering.*
>
> **Laura Kittell**

★ Use props and visuals on radio shows. The host can describe them to the audience. For instance, the radio person could say, "I'm holding in my hand an example of the networking card you created. This is the most bizarre thing I've ever seen. Tell me about it." That enhances radio interviews.

Call-in Shows

Live shows allow people in the audience to call and talk to you personally. Welcome the opportunity to perform under these conditions. It makes for a more interesting show, and if there are many callers, the host is more likely to invite you back for a repeat performance.

Although most callers are screened beforehand, you have no control over what the callers will ask. Their inquiries will run the gamut from off-the-wall questions having nothing to do with what you are talking about to pertinent questions dealing directly with your topic. Some will even take exception to your comments. But all this makes a good radio show.

> *I love the edge, not knowing who is going to call or what they're going to say. Always stay calm and let the host deal with irrational callers.*
> **Eric Marcus**

You may get an abusive caller, but the host is there to protect you. If the abuse is directed at you personally, the host will normally cut off the caller. But if the controversy is about your topic or position, the host will usually let the two of you discuss it within the bounds of decorum. No matter how much you want to berate the caller, do not do it. Be polite, explain your points and speak eloquently.

> *In terms of belligerent callers, it depends entirely on the nature of the belligerence. If it's a personal assault, it's the host's job to avoid it. If it's a subject of legitimate concern, and the caller brings a certain passion to the topic, then I just let the guest and caller mix it up. If the guest has written a book on anything that approaches controversy, he or she must be aware of the fact that controversy will arise.*
> **Jim Bohannon**

Get the audience involved in your discussion and it will be more likely to call you. Do that by offering a prize (your book) to the first caller who answers your question correctly. This technique also gets your book's title mentioned more frequently without you being pushy.

> *The more involved your answer, the less involved is your audience. They think, "I can't do all that" and they'll tune you out. Make it sound easy for them.*
> **Suzi Reynolds**

Another idea is to offer an analysis of a major news event and request people with the opposite view to call and explain their position. As the listeners hear you respond with an open mind to callers, others will be more likely to call.

Don't shoot from the lip

After appearing on several radio shows, you will be able to anticipate many of the questions the callers will ask. Yet, in most cases it is difficult to have a stock answer because each one will contain an individual concern. Your challenge is to turn a question into a platform to discuss one of your agenda items.

Here are several guidelines that will help make each call-in show a pleasant experience:

☎ Before the show, ask friends and relatives to call in. Give them the station's studio number (which is usually different from the main number) and questions to ask relating to your agenda. Many people do not like to be the first to call, and your *plant* will break the ice.

☎ The host may give you a headset so you can hear the caller. Do not be frightened or annoyed that your hair will get messed up (remember, this is radio and people cannot see you). Use the headset and you will be surprised at how much clearer the voices will be.

☎ Keep a note pad with you. As the caller gives his or her name, note and mention it during the call. Also, jot down key words to which you can refer while answering. Listen to the entire question for a familiar word you can use to make the transition to one of your agenda items (which may or may not be the point of the question).

On my show, the same type of answers you would give the host you would give the caller.
Jim Bohannon

62 Special Hints for Performing on Radio Shows

☎ If you need more information to answer properly, ask the caller to expand on the question. The more the caller talks, the more likely you are to find the one familiar point on which you can base your answer. Use reflective statements ("Oh really? Tell me more.") to keep the caller talking.

☎ You may find it helpful to rephrase the question. This will make sure you are addressing the underlying meaning, and it gives you the chance to restate it, making it easier to answer. Repeat the question, perhaps making the transition into your agenda. Then say, "Is that what you were referring to?"

> *If you have people calling in to the show, you have to engage them and ask them questions.*
> **Eric Marcus**

☎ If you are asked two questions simultaneously, choose the order in which you will answer them. Answer the easier question first, then ask for the other to be repeated. This not only gives you time to think, but the second question may be answered in the process, or forgotten.

☎ Always be courteous and never belittle a caller. Make something interesting out of what you think is a frivolous question by saying, "That's an interesting point, especially if you consider this aspect of it ...." If the question was already covered (perhaps before this caller tuned in), mention it and briefly summarize your previous answer. If you can add something to what you said earlier, do so.

☎ Make each caller sound important. If appropriate, remark, "That's a good question." Pause briefly, as if pondering your reply, and then proceed with your response.

☎ Some callers may seek their 15 minutes of fame by trying to trip you up. Maintain your composure and use your grasp of the facts and figures to back up your comments. Do not try to prove a questioner wrong; prove yourself right by citing your research.

> *A healthy clash of ideas in of itself may very well help sell your book.*
>
> **Jim Bohannon**

☎ Do not lose your self-control and do not argue with a caller. State your case professionally and back up your remarks with facts. Tell irate callers you understand what they are saying without agreeing with them. If a caller becomes argumentative or profane, the host will usually cut him or her off.

> *Some of the best advice I ever got was, "Always say it with a smile." Be nice even if it kills you.*
>
> **Eric Marcus**

☎ Remember your agenda and do not allow yourself to be led astray. Avoid confrontational issues not related to your objectives.

☎ If you do not know the answer, admit it. If the question is out of your area of expertise, tell the caller where he or she can find the answer.

☎ Visualize the caller and talk to *him* or *her*. Make it sound as if the two of you are sitting in a living room having a friendly conversation.

> *We're just talking. The rest of the country is eaves-dropping, but don't think of them. They're really not out there as far as you are concerned. We're just here and one or two of our friends will call in and talk on the radio.*
>
> **Jim Bohannon**

Telephone Interviews

You can use your telephone to tape radio shows or perform live, from any place in which there is a good connection, no background noise and where you can talk uninterrupted for the length of the show. Telephone interviews provide inexpensive exposure because the producer will call you, typically. You may be asked to call the station or asked to pay for the privilege of being a guest, but this happens rarely. In such cases, before agreeing to perform weigh the benefits of exposure on the show versus the cost.

> *I don't think a tour always works. I don't think it al-ways makes sense to make that kind of investment. There is a lot you can do from home that doesn't cost as much as a tour. One of the things I discovered that turned out to be the most productive was simply doing telephone interviews from my own home.*
>
> **Eric Marcus**

You may find yourself doing ten or more telephone interviews per week. This can feed your ego if you think about the millions of people around the country who will have heard you.

> *You can do 100 radio shows all across the country and never leave your home. It's a beautiful thing.*
> **Rick Frishman**

But one show in a city does not make a big impression, so do not get carried away thinking you are creating a national reputation. Telephone interviews are a good first step in that direction, but you need reach *and* frequency so people remember your title long enough to go out and buy your book. Here are several guidelines to make telephone interviews more effective:

☎ As you agree upon the time and date with the producer, confirm your time zone. The producer may say he or she will call you at 3:00, but is that 3:00 p.m. your time or show time? Will he or she call you at the top of the hour or after the news is finished? The time spent waiting between 3:00 and 3:06 increases your nervousness and you will begin to question if you have the right day, and time, or if you were to call the studio at 3:00.

☎ Do not use cellular telephones and do not ask the station to call you on a line with call waiting. That familiar clicking sound will interfere with the continuity of the show. Similarly, this is not the time to impress your friends by having them listen to you on an extension or speaker phone.

☎ Have a specific area set aside for telephone interviews, one in which you can keep your notes, books and pad handy. Unplug nearby phones if they are on a different line. Close the door and place an "On The Air" sign on it to eliminate unintentional interruptions. Have fun with your radio interviews.

> *Once I did an interview from the lobby of an inn in southern Maine when I was at a wedding.*
>
> **Eric Marcus**

☎ Do not be concerned if the connection is not perfect. If the studio personnel cannot compensate for extraneous noise, they will call you back. However, if you find it difficult to hear, ask them to call you again. Otherwise, you will have to press the telephone tightly against your ear (causing discomfort) or ask the host to repeat questions.

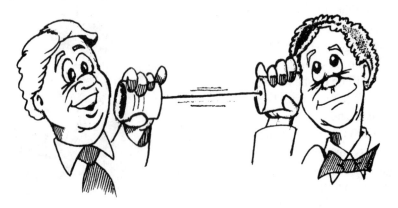

☎ Nobody will say, "You're on the air," so always assume the microphone is hot (live). You can hear the change in sound when you go live, but do not take any chances. Speak only when spoken to and do all your voice exercises beforehand, not while you are on hold.

☎ Your host may want to give the audience the impression that you are in the studio. He or she may say, "Here with us today is Brian Jud, author of *Job Search 101.*" Take the hint and do not make comments such as, "How's the weather out there?" Most will say that you are out of town, connected by telephone, giving you more credibility as a busy, sought-after author.

☎ In order to create a prestigious image, you will be introduced as the expert on your topic. Play up to that representation, projecting an aura of competence and knowledge. The audience wants to learn something from a credible source, and you are that person.

☎ While you are on hold, either before you begin the interview or during a break, you will hear the station's regular programming. Listen for key points to which you can refer later. On long shows, the host may talk to you during the break to plan what you will discuss during the next segment.

☎ Give your ears a rest. Alternate the telephone from one ear to the other during lengthy segments. If you have a speaker phone, engage it *during the breaks only*. Purchase a headset if you participate in telephone interviews frequently. It will free your hands to write. And if you gesture normally, do so during your radio interviews so you will feel comfortable emphasizing your words.

☎ Before a long show starts, ask when breaks will occur and how long each will be. Buy a clock with a large second hand so you can gauge the timing of your answers as the breaks approach. Listen for the show's theme music, which will usually start at low volume and increase as it leads to the break. Close your answer as the music begins.

☎ Keep water nearby and drink it generously, but only during breaks so the sound of your swallowing is not heard on the air (and if the water goes down the wrong pipe, your coughing will not interfere with your interview). If you must cough, place your hand over the mouthpiece. Do not drink anything alcoholic.

☎ Keep your list of questions and answers in front of you. Refer to it regularly and make notes as you speak. Make all your planned agenda points before concluding.

☎ After two or three shows in one day, you may begin to wonder if you are repeating yourself. Make notes as you speak to remind yourself of what you said earlier. If you use acronyms to prompt your reply, list them on a pad and cross off each as you discuss it.

☎ Write the host's name phonetically at the top of your note pad and use it during the show. Writing it will reduce the chances of calling him or her by the wrong name if you conduct several interviews with different people in one day.

☎ Sit in a comfortable, quiet chair. If you gesture frequently, try standing as you speak. Keep your head high to open your breathing passages; relax your jaw muscles and you will speak more clearly.

☎ Laura Kittell suggests you keep a mirror in front of you as you speak. Keep a smile on your face and you will have a smile in your voice.

☎ Do not schedule telephone interviews too closely together. Invariably, one will be delayed due to an unpredictable event, perhaps impinging on the time allocated to another show.

☎ Rarely will you get bumped (canceled on short notice), but it can happen. If so, be polite and reschedule your show for another time.

☎ At the end of the show, you will get the chance to tell the listeners where they can find your book. If your toll-free number spells out a word, give both the pronunciation and the numbers. For example, if the toll-free number is 1 (800) JOB - HELP, say it and then repeat the numbers: "That's 1 (800) 562-4357."

> *Give listeners an incentive to call. For example, you can say, "Call this 800 number to order my book and I will send a free report." You've just given them more of a reason to drop everything and order today.*
>
> **Steve Hall**

Sometimes people are listening to the radio while driving and do not have a pencil and paper nearby. Encourage them to write down your toll-free number by letting them know ahead of time. Say, "In a few minutes I'll give you the name and address of an organization where you can obtain a free credit report." Listeners will be prepared when the time comes to give them your toll-free number.

Similarly, it is easier to remember a post office box number than a street address. If your box number can be misconstrued, make it clear. Your P. O. Box 9D may sound like "90." Say, "Box 9 D as in Dog." Also, spell out and repeat the name of your town if necessary, and give only a 5-digit zip code rather than the full 9-digit number.

Handle your hang-ups well

Do not be upset if you are disconnected abruptly after a telephone interview without a word of thanks. The host has to move on to the next guest or back to the regular programming and will not always have time to thank you. Instead of

getting angry, immediately evaluate your performance and plan what you can do differently and better next time.

If you are thorough in your preparation, you will alert your host to your potential as an interesting guest. You both will be relaxed, and the interview will be conducted between two professionals, both trying to create an interesting, informative and entertaining show to meet their respective objectives. When this occurs, you will be asked back to repeat your performance.

> *People respect those who are discrete and style them-selves in a good-mannered way. Over-promoting your-self is a negative on a radio talk show.*
>
> **Larry Kahn**

Chapter Eight

SPECIAL HINTS FOR PERFORMING ON TELEVISION

Television is the glamour medium in the broadcast industry, making you instantly recognizable to millions of people across the country. You can reach them in one day during a performance on a national show, a task that would take hundreds of thousands of dollars to do with paid commercial time.

> *An interview on television is the perfect format for an author to get his or her advertising going, to get their word-of-mouth going and to get his or her story told.*
>
> **Brad Hurtado**

As you can imagine, there is tremendous competition among people to appear on these shows. Producers can choose from a wide variety of potential guests, and they want to be certain their choice is a good one. The deciding factor is: What people and topics will most interest the show's audience?

> *What does your book mean to other people? That's what you talk about.*
>
> **Suzi Reynolds**

Final Preparation

When you arrive at the television studio, you will be shown to a waiting area known as the *green room*. There, the producer or host will introduce him- or herself to you and discuss the general direction of the show. This is primarily a time to get to know each other. Also, use it to ask any questions you have about what is going to happen. If you have props or visuals to show on the air, describe how you will use them so the producer can arrange the best camera angle. If you have a book signing or other event coming up, tell the producer and he or she can put the time and place on the screen.

> *Ask them to make a full screen. Say, "I will be at the ABC Book Store tomorrow at 2 o'clock. Can we get that in?"*
>
> **Benita Zahn**

The qualm before the storm

Just before it is time to go on the air, visit the rest room one last time. Check the mirror to inspect your makeup and hair. Adjust your clothes and remove anything wedged between your teeth. Make sure your zipper is up and return to the green room to await your call. Breath deeply and relax. Continue watching the show on the monitor to get a feel for the personality of the show and the host's interviewing style.

Local shows may give you the opportunity to get on the set before your time arrives. If so, walk in and mentally take possession of it. This will help you feel at ease and your body will begin to align with the temperature. If you tend to perspire, it will give your body time to adjust.

> *The biggest fears people have when they come into the studio is they'll look foolish, that they're not going to know what to do and not know where to put themselves. All you have to worry about is being comfortable. If you're not comfortable, you won't do well answering the questions. Sit down and feel at home. Talk to the interviewer. Ask, "What should I do? Who should I look at?" Ask if everything is in place. They'll tell you.*
>
> **Benita Zahn**

Soon you will be led to the studio, and someone will show you to your seat. A microphone will be clipped on your clothes in the appropriate spot, usually high up on the same side of your body as the host is sitting. This assures that you will be speaking into the microphone as you face him or her. Do not blow into it to see if it is working.

> *The microphone is not your responsibility. They'll make sure it's hooked up right. But you might want to look down, once the mike is in place, to make sure there are no wires hanging out.*
> **Rita Thompson**

A voice-level check will be performed, usually as you and the host are talking. When asked, look at the host and speak as you will during your performance. Once the host squares up with the camera, do not say anything else until you are asked.

As the show starts or commercial concludes, you will hear the show's theme music. The floor director or camera operator will count down from five on his or her fingers and then point to the host. He or she will begin to introduce you, generally reading from a prepared script. A segment typically starts with a close-up of the host as you are being introduced. The camera then moves to an establishing shot, showing the viewers how the host and guest are positioned. In moments, the red light on your camera brightens and *you're on the air!*

Relax and make the event an enjoyable experience. Talk to the host in a lively, entertaining fashion. Be engaging, informative and talk in sound bites. If the host wants to develop a point any further, he or she will ask you.

> *The most important thing is to have fun, relax. This is only television, it's not a big deal. Have a good time.*
> **Lori Dolney Levine**

Delivering Your Message Visually

All the previously described techniques of verbal and vocal delivery apply to your television appearances, too. But now you have a new dimension to deal with: your visual presentation. You have to look and act the part of a knowledgeable and confident guest.

There is no second chance to make a good first impression, and your initial impression upon the audience is made by the way you look. Do you appear to be a credible source of information, one whom it should continue watching?

There are three major elements that control the way you are perceived by the viewers initially. These are your physical features, clothes and body language:

1) There's not much you can do to change your physical features, but you can work with them.

★ Bright studio lights are necessary to make the set appear natural, but they have the opposite effect on people. They highlight complexion blemishes and can create sinister-looking dark circles under eyes set back in one's head.

It's a cover-up!

Use makeup to hide or accentuate certain physical features. Most women use makeup regularly and feel comfortable wearing it. If you are not familiar or comfortable with makeup, get assistance from your spouse, media trainer or from a sales representative at a local theatrical or cosmetic shop. Learn how to apply it yourself because in most cases there will not be a professional on staff to do it for you.

If you know you look good you'll be more confident.
Suzi Reynolds

Use makeup with a water-base foundation to keep your skin from becoming oily under the hot lights. If your makeup irritates you, there are nonallergenic brands available.

As you choose your lipstick and blusher, remember the studio lights give off a blue cast making dark blue appear black and reds look redder. After the show, remove your makeup with soap and water. The lights will dry out your skin, so use a moisturizer to replace normal body oil.

> *For women, wear what you're used to wearing. Put on the same makeup as you always do. Nothing garish, but something you would normally wear as street makeup. For men, powder your face, just a little to cover a receding hairline and tone your face down so you won't be shiny.*
>
> **Benita Zahn**

★ Lose or gain weight if necessary. Closeup images can make you appear heavier than you are.

★ Have your hair cut to your specifications two weeks before your appearance. Get that manicure you have always wanted. Shave and trim any facial hair (including your eyebrows to help prevent shadows forming around your eyes). Men should carry an electric shaver with them to touch up their beard late in the day.

★ Sleep well the night before so your eyes do not appear bloodshot.

2) Dress to feel comfortable and create the image you want.

★ Choose clothes that will not distract from your message. People should pay attention to what you say, not what you are wearing.

Visually communicate and reinforce one message: you are a credible source of interesting and important information for the people in your target market.

★ Look the part you are trying to convey. Is it a wealthy businessperson? Then you will probably wear a tailored suit. A fitness expert? Then workout attire may be the appropriate choice.

★ Wear something on which you can pin a microphone if the studio is not using a boom or hand-held sound system.

★ Choose colors that are best for you, given your hair and skin coloring. In general, dark colors are best for suits, and blue is a safe color. Earth tones and neutral colors work well on television, too. Before you choose your attire for any particular show, watch it or call ahead to find out the background color of the set.

★ There are certain colors and combinations to avoid. In all cases, shun solid white. This causes hot spots for the camera, preventing it from focusing properly. For similar reasons, do not wear satin. Instead, wear light blue which appears white under the lights. And since cotton wrinkles significantly, you may want to consider blends. Avoid anything close to herringbone, narrow pinstripes or tight plaids because the cameras cannot focus on them.

★ Men should wear over-the-calf socks and pants long enough to cover them when you cross your legs. Women should not wear a short skirt that might ride up during the show.

> *For men, the odds are you're going to be unbuttoning your jacket. For women, you may unbutton the bottom just so it lays nice and smooth.*
> **Benita Zahn**

★ Due to the combination of your general apprehension and hot lights, wearing wool may cause you to perspire more. Most studios are temperature controlled to compensate for the heat given off by the lights, but as Murphy's Law would have it, you will eventually find yourself on a warm set without air conditioning. Keep a handkerchief with you and pat your face dry when the camera is not on you. Do not wipe the perspiration or you will smear your makeup.

> *Unless you perspire heavily, it's not going to show. You'll just glisten a little.*
> **Benita Zahn**

★ Accessories should be simple, nondistracting and quiet. Use them to complement your intended image. Jewelry should be functional, subtle and not so bright as to cause camera problems. Shoes should be shined and free from holes in the bottom.

★ Glasses may be worn if needed to read; however, this is not the time to try your new contact lenses. Photosensitive eyeglasses turn dark under the lights and may portray a sinister image. Do not wear them unless they are part of your identification. Keep glasses and pens out of your jacket pocket, or they will distract the viewer from your message.

3) **There are volumes written about body language and how you project an image through your posture, movements and gestures, intentionally or unintentionally.** Since the bulk of your believability is projected visually, you can control your image by manipulating your body language.

Mind your mannerisms

★ Slumped posture can contradict your assertions of self-confidence. Sit up straight at all times.

> *Smile. It brings your face up, your eyes up and even brings your posture up.*
>
> **Suzi Reynolds**

★ At the same time, be seated comfortably with your forearms placed on the arm rests. Sit toward the front of the chair and lean slightly forward. If you are seated in a large sofa, sit near the front edge so you are not enveloped in it, particularly if you are short.

> *The simplest thing is to keep your hands in your lap, since most people are comfortable with that.*
>
> **Rita Thompson**

★ Unfortunately, you can not tell by the camera's position whether the actual image is a closeup or not, so create a mental frame within which you can motion. Practice gesturing slowly, within the bounds of your upper body. Anything outside this frame will not be seen, even in a medium camera shot.

★ Use your hands strategically and naturally. Do not use quick, stiff, contrived gestures, but practice making smooth ones that appear spontaneous. Use your hands and arms to reinforce what you are saying. Use your fingers to tick off points or emphasize your agenda items. Point your finger only to direct focal attention, and never at the host or camera. And do not touch your face. This projects insincerity, hides your face and could possibly smear your makeup.

> *If you're comfortable with gestures, do gestures. If you're not comfortable with them, don't. But if you want to talk with your hands, talk with them; otherwise, you won't be able to think.*
>
> **Benita Zahn**

★ Poets have called eyes the mirror of the soul because your eye contact (or lack thereof) will do more to communicate your true self than almost anything else you can do.

★ Do not look into the camera as you answer the interviewer's questions. You are having a discussion with your host, so focus on his or her eyes. Break contact periodically so you do not lock eyes and stare at the host constantly. To get a feel for the appropriate amount of time to hold contact, try this technique: as you are introduced, look into the person's eyes long enough so you can describe the color of his or her eyes to yourself.

★ A closeup camera shot will exaggerate your eye movements, so do not dart or blink quickly. Look downward momentarily to collect your thoughts, but do not break contact at a crucial time (such as during an intense panel discussion), or you may communicate the perception of lack of confidence.

★ Some shows use more closeup shots than others. If your target show uses tight camera shots, remember to gesture more slowly and minimize dramatic facial expressions which are unbecoming in a closeup.

Don't worry about facial gestures, that you think you have to make them bigger. You don't. Television makes everything bigger. Working in a small environment, every eyebrow now looks like a mountain moving.

Benita Zahn

★ Combine eye communication with facial and head movements. For example, if you must bear down upon another panel member with sustained eye communication, smile as you do so to thwart a negative response from viewers.

What helps sometimes is to look down and look up. People don't stare into the eyes of another person they're talking to. So if you need a moment to regroup, look down, look up and keep going.

Lori Dolney Levine

★ A good guest also knows how to read the host's body language to know when it is time for a transition. For example, when the host signals your segment is coming to a close, you should begin to summarize your main points.

> *Look for the clues that the interviewers are giving you.*
> *They may gesture to let you know they're getting ready*
> *for another question or for another guest to join in the*
> *conversation.*
>
> **Larry Kahn**

Prop up your performance

If you have props or visuals that will strengthen or clarify your information, use them. But use only those that will enhance or further what you are saying.

> *You can really increase your chances of being booked*
> *on a television talk show if you have visuals that you can*
> *show people.*
>
> **Steve Hall**

When you bring your props to the studio, check with the producer before the show starts so he or she will know what kind and size visuals you are talking about. Discuss where to put them and practice using them before the show starts. Ask which camera will be on them and from what angles and distances they will be shot. Will you have to lift or just point to your props? Keep in mind that shiny props and small pictures do not do well on television. Get all your visuals to work for, not against, you.

> *The perfect guest on television is someone who believes*
> *in his topic, can answer concisely and can sit nice and*
> *steady.*
>
> **Benita Zahn**

Chapter Nine

AFTER THE SHOW

Once your interview is over, do not stand up immediately. Wait for an indication that the camera has stopped rolling and for someone to remove your microphone.

EVALUATION

If the show will continue after your segment, politely excuse yourself and leave. But if the show ends with your segment, spend some time with your host(s). Ask for suggestions that will help you improve. If the host says you performed well, ask if you can use his or her quotation in your future promotion. If you revise your promotional material to include the host's quotation, send him or her a copy.

> *Sit down until told to get up and never take the microphone with you. You're not allowed to take souvenirs.*
> **Benita Zahn**

As you drive home, evaluate your performance. Note the questions which caught you off guard and practice ways to answer them.

★ As soon as possible, send thank-you notes to the host and producer of the show. Let them know you are willing to serve as a guest on short notice, if they should have a last-minute cancellation.

★ Add everyone's name to your mailing list and update each producer with your promotional information regularly. People in broadcast media change jobs frequently, and their move to another station might pave the way for you to become a guest on it.

★ Add the words "As seen on television" to your literature.

★ Send a summary monthly of your appearances to your distributors, wholesalers and major buyers.

★ Update your press kit. List all major shows on which you have appeared, and use your revised kit to recontact all the shows that turned you down previously.

Checklists for *It's Show Time*

Evaluate all your performances. Watch and study them. Although you should not be too hard on yourself, evaluate the tapes of the shows objectively. Do not automatically begin by looking for what you did wrong. It is important to know both the good and bad parts of any situation so you can evaluate it with perspective.

After every interview, go through the following checklists to evaluate where you went right. Think about what you could do differently next time, and then assess how you could improve upon what you did incorrectly.

Before the show did you:
❑ take media training?
❑ reread your book and highlight important facts?
❑ become familiar with your table of contents and subheadings?
❑ become familiar with issues not in your book?
❑ learn about late-breaking news stories relating to your topic?
❑ list your ten most important topics, ranked in order of importance?
❑ construct transition statements that will focus on your agenda items?
❑ develop examples to make agenda items relevant and interesting?
❑ plan acronyms and comparisons?
❑ spend enough time practicing?
❑ call the producer/host to confirm the date and time beforehand?
❑ learn the names of the other panel members?
❑ give the producer a blank tape on which to copy the show?
❑ listen to the radio show while driving to it?
❑ perform relaxation exercises on the way to the show?
❑ create and use positive affirmations?
❑ greet the producer and host confidently?
❑ ask questions about unfamiliar equipment and people?
❑ tell the host how to describe you during the introduction?

While performing on the air did you:
❑ relax and have fun?
❑ use the hosts's name frequently enough?
❑ prepare for the show and answer all questions creatively?
❑ use examples that were credible and convincing?
❑ answer all questions completely? Did you ramble?
❑ weave current or local issues into your answers?
❑ give clear and concise answers to all questions?
❑ discuss your topic from the viewpoint of the people in the audience?
❑ use your VOICES properly?
❑ organize your presentation to make it more interesting and effective?
❑ participate in the interview actively?
❑ anticipate the questions sufficiently?
❑ listen carefully to the host?

During radio shows did you:
- ❏ speak into the microphone?
- ❏ use your notes effectively without searching for information?
- ❏ have your friends call and ask questions?
- ❏ interact well with the callers?

During television shows did you:
- ❏ dress to make a good first impression?
- ❏ apply your makeup properly?
- ❏ bring props and use them effectively?
- ❏ maintain eye contact with the host?
- ❏ eliminate distracting accessories?
- ❏ use eye communication effectively? How can you improve?
- ❏ use body language effectively? How can you improve?

After the show did you:
- ❏ think about how you can improve your performance next time?
- ❏ follow up and send thank-you notes?

Appearing on radio or television is a rewarding experience, both personally and professionally. If you prepare and relax, you will succeed and enjoy yourself. Each successive show will be easier, more fun and more profitable for you, the media and the audience. Your performances will be win/win/win propositions for everyone, and you will reach whatever goals you have set for yourself.

> *People respond to regular people. Nobody in the audience wants to think that you've arrived and now you're beyond their reach, now you're a celebrity and you're above them. The greatest asset you have is that you're one of them. You're somebody who began with a problem and you overcame it. You've got to strike those chords, touch those nerves. How do you make people fall in love with you? Be real, substantive and know your stuff.*
> **Suzi Reynolds**

Index

Order Form

You're On The Air. A 90-minute video program employing interviews with the producers of top national talk shows to demonstrate techniques for performing successfully on television and radio. It is a media performance and voice training course combined in one information-packed videotape.

It's Show Time. This companion guide to *You're On The Air* complements the information about performing on television and radio, reinforced by advice and quotes from the talk-show hosts and producers.

Perpetual Promotion. The informative, complete 100-page book describes how to organize your own promotional tour. It tells you where to find the names of the producers who decide who gets on the air and who does not. How to create an effective press kit, how to get producers' attention, and how to follow up without aggravating them are some of the questions addressed in detail.

Please send this order form to the Publisher, Marketing Directions, Inc., P. O. Box 715, Avon, CT 06001-0715, (800) 562-4357, fax (860) 676-0759. For more information go to: http://www.marketingdirections.com.

Please send me:

_____ copies of *You're On The Air* @ $89.95 + $4.95 S&H $ _____

_____ copies of *It's Show Time* @ $14.95 + $1.50 S&H $ _____

_____ copies of *Perpetual Promotion* @ $14.95 + $1.50 S&H $ _____

_____ sets of all three items @ $99.95 + $5.95 S&H $ _____

Order total $ _____

CT residents add 6% sales tax $ _____

Total enclosed $ _____

Name _____

Address _____

City _____

State _____ Zip Code _____

Telephone ( ) _____

Visa/MasterCard number: _____

Expiration Date: _____

Signature: _____